.... WHAT'S AT ISSUE? ....

SCIENCE & YOU

David Applin

Heinemann
LIBRARY

H **www.heinemann.co.uk/library**
Visit our website to find out more information about **Heinemann Library** books.

To order:
☎ Phone 44 (0) 1865 888066
📄 Send a fax to 44 (0) 1865 314091
💻 Visit the Heinemann Bookshop at www.heinemann.co.uk/library to browse our catalogue and order online.

First published in Great Britain by Heinemann Library, Halley Court, Jordan Hill, Oxford OX2 8EJ, a division of Reed Educational and Professional Publishing Ltd. Heinemann is a registered trademark of Reed Educational & Professional Publishing Limited.

OXFORD MELBOURNE AUCKLAND JOHANNESBURG BLANTYRE
GABORONE IBADAN PORTSMOUTH NH (USA) CHICAGO

Designed by Tinstar Design (www.tinstar.co.uk)
Originated by Ambassador Litho Ltd
Printed in Hong Kong/China

ISBN 0 431 03557 1   (hardback)   ISBN 0 431 03565 2   (paperback)
06 05 04 03 02   06 05 04 03 02
10 9 8 7 6 5 4 3 2   10 9 8 7 6 5 4 3 2 1

British Library Cataloguing in Publication Data
Applin, David
    Science & You. – (What's at issue?)
    1. Science & You – Juvenile literature 2. Immorality –
    Juvenile literature
    I. Title
    170

Acknowledgements
For Joan Applin, beloved mother, grandmother, wife and companion whose example inspired a love of scholarship and learning.

The Publishers would like to thank the following for permission to reproduce photographs:
Corbis: p26, Smithsonian Museum, USA p4, Peter Turnley p20, Paul Velasco p29, Bettmann p30, Francis G Mayer p34, Paul A Sowders p36, Liba Taylor p41; David Applin: p28; Hulton Getty: p38; Photdisc: pp37, 42; Popperfoto: p19, Reuters p13; Rex Features: Paul Rogers p14, Nick Cobbing p22, David Allocca p43; Science Photo Library: A Barrington Brown p6, BSIP/Laurent p7, Saturn Stills p9, Garry Watson p10, JL Martra, Publiphoto Diffusion p16, Jim Gipe/Agstock p18, P Marazzi p32, Richard Nowitz p35; Tony Stone Images: Charles Thatcher p40; Tudor Photography: pp24, 39

Cover photograph: Rex Features.

Our thanks to Robert Snedden for his comments in the preparation of this book.

Every effort has been made to contact copyright holders of any material reproduced in this book. Any omissions will be rectified in subsequent printings if notice is given to the Publisher.

Any words appearing in the text in bold, **like this**, are explained in the Glossary.

Contents

Introduction

We live in an age of science, with announcements of inventions and new discoveries making the headlines almost every day. Even supermarket products – microwave meals, biological washing liquids, long-life foods – come from the application of science.

In 1939 a German scientist called Otto Hahn split the atom. His discovery opened the way to a source of unlimited energy with which to power industry and our homes. But it also led to the horror of the atom bomb, dropped on Hiroshima and Nagasaki in 1945. The twin blasts killed tens of thousands of people and gave countless survivors the deadly effects of radiation for the rest of their lives.

Science – for good or for ill? The answers are in our hands. *Science and You* helps you ask the questions which explore today's scientific issues.

Understanding evolution

Have you ever wondered why there are so many different types of bird? About 155 million years ago early types of bird were flying the skies but there weren't as many types as there are now. These early birds differed in appearance and behaviour from each other because their **genes** also differed. Some birds were perhaps suited to pounce on prey, others to eating berries. The individuals with the most suitable characteristics for their environment (those able to pounce on more prey or eat more berries) were more likely to survive and reproduce but the others died out. The genes controlling these survival characteristics were then inherited by their offspring. The process is called **natural selection**.

The characteristics which help individuals to survive gradually change as the environment in which they live changes. The changes usually take place over many generations. The birds we see today are adapted to their environment, and early types of bird such as *Archaeopteryx* have died out. This process of change is called evolution. It means that present day living things are descended from **ancestors** that looked or behaved differently from them.

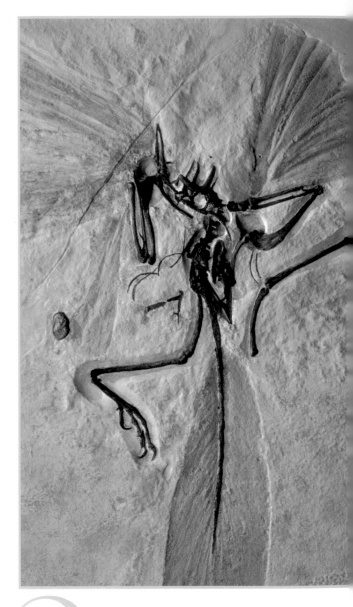

This fossil from the Jurassic period shows the *Archaeopteryx* – the oldest known bird.

Enter Charles Darwin

Most people link the British naturalist Charles Darwin (1809–82) with the theory of evolution. However, the idea was an old one – the Greek philosopher Aristotle (384–322 BC) argued the case for evolution. Darwin's contribution to the theory was to identify natural selection as the mechanism of evolution. In other words he explained how living things evolve.

Alfred Russel Wallace

Darwin worked for many years on his theory that evolution occurred through natural selection. He was cautious about publishing it, perhaps because he thought his ideas would attract fierce criticism from people who believed the biblical story about the creation of the world and life. However, in 1858 he was shocked to receive from the naturalist Alfred Russel Wallace (1823–1913) a letter and essay in which Wallace outlined the idea that natural selection was the mechanism for evolutionary change. For Darwin, it was a terrible blow. He had worked patiently on the same idea for many years, yet Wallace had come to the same conclusion. Darwin discussed the matter with a few close friends and fellow scientists. It was agreed that Darwin and Wallace should jointly publish their ideas in the *Journal of the Linnean Society* for 1858. A year later, in 1859, Darwin published his book *The Origin of Species* and nervously awaited the public's reaction.

Issues of belief

In general people believe something is true if the evidence seems to prove the case or if the idea fits into the **moral** framework by which they live day-to-day. Each generation asks 'Who are we?', 'What are we?' and 'Why do we exist?' For many people, their religion helps answer the questions, but evolution seems to contradict religion. People's responses to the contradictions were probably what Darwin feared most when *The Origin of Species* was published.

Today, the theory of evolution remains controversial. For many people with strong religious beliefs, evolution is unproven. They argue that evolution has never been seen to happen and that no one was present when life first appeared on Earth.

Other people, some who hold strong religious beliefs (and are also scientists), point out that we are surrounded by the

OPPOSING VIEWS

In 1859 in Britain, most people were Christians and believed the stories of the Bible to be the literal truth. They thought that God had created the world and opposed Darwin's theory that life on Earth was a result of evolution. Today creationists still oppose the views of scientists whose work supports Darwin's theory. For them, creation theory based on biblical evidence contradicts the scientific evidence.

Creationists

According to the Bible, God created his own image in Adam from the dust of the world. Before Adam's creation, night was separated from day and the world was formed of water and dry land. Living things were created to live in water and on land, and once created remained the same forever. It took God six days to achieve The Creation. On the seventh day he rested.

Scientists

If most scientists are correct, planet Earth formed from the dust and gases circling a star we call the sun around 4500 million years ago. Evidence suggests that about 500 million years later, the first stirrings of life on Earth occurred. Present-day living things evolved through countless generations from these early forms of life.

In what ways do you think the views of scientists and creationists are opposed to one another?

results of evolution – life on Earth – and that there are some cases of evolutionary change which we can see. The development of resistance by bacteria to antibiotic drugs, which are designed to attack the bacteria that cause disease, is an example. The issues raise important questions for society. In the USA, for example, teachers have been prosecuted for teaching evolution.

The human genome

On 28 February 1953, James Watson and Francis Crick realized that they had discovered the secret of life. Their discovery was the structure of **DNA** and it sparked a scientific revolution.

DNA is a substance that nearly all **organisms** have. It contains four substances called bases – Adenine, Cytosine, Guanine and Thymine, or A, C, G and T. These bases are part of the building blocks that make up a length of DNA.

Genes are made of short segments of very long DNA **molecules**. These DNA molecules are coiled and folded around **proteins** to form **chromosomes**. The **nucleus** of each human cell contains 46 chromosomes, except sperm and eggs, which contain 23. The chromosomes are the cell's genetic material. The genes on the chromosomes convert the instructions into code that cells need to do their jobs. An especially important job for any cell is to make different types of protein.

The sequence (ordering) of the bases A, C, G and T gives the instruction code for making a particular type of protein. A different sequence of those letters instructs the cell to make another type of protein. In this way the different proteins that all living things need to grow, build and repair their bodies are made. Watson and Crick's work was the first vital step in understanding this **blueprint** for human life.

The American biologist James Watson (left) and the British physicist Francis Crick (right) and their model of DNA. The model looks like a ladder twisted into a spiral shape, called a double helix, which is why DNA is sometimes called the double helix.

Reading the sequence

The word genome means all of the genes in an organism. After years of research, thousands of scientists working together on a project called HUGO (Human Genome Organization) in laboratories across the world have worked out the first rough outline of the human genome. The process began with the gathering of cell samples (blood and sperm) taken from anonymous volunteers. Scientists broke up the chromosomes of the cells into pieces to get at their DNA. The lengths of DNA from each chromosome contain the genes which scientists have worked to decode. Thousands of copies of the lengths of DNA were made to provide enough material for the decoding work, which involved detailing the sequence of As, Cs, Gs and Ts. Computer technology has been vital in speeding up the decoding process.

Whose genome is it?

The code of the human genome is being fought over by two kinds of scientists – those who receive money from governments and those who are funded by private businesses. The prize is the development of new medicines and treatments which come from knowing the genetic causes of disease. The different genetic causes of cancer are a major target. Scientists receiving public funds argue that information which is in effect about our biology should be available to everyone. Scientists receiving private funds say that the investment of millions of pounds and dollars into work on the human genome must be protected by **patents**. This would mean that private business would control the invention or discovery.

Many people find it shocking that ownership of parts of the genome should be in the hands of a few individuals who run genome companies and the **shareholders** who invest in them. But spokespeople for the companies say that unless patents exist there is no encouragement for investors to make money available for scientific progress. Without the possibility of profits from new medicines and treatments, why should people risk their money?

Other issues might arise from a greater understanding of our genes. Will people who are known to have faulty genes, which increase their risk of suffering from serious illness, be able to obtain insurance or a mortgage to buy a home? Will governments choose to set up a national database that allows individuals to be identified genetically for whatever reason, innocent or otherwise? The possibilities are endless. What are your views?

Scientists can now read the sequence of the human genome.

Genetic testing

Children inherit their **chromosomes** and **genes** from their mother and father. As a result, faulty genes and the diseases they cause are often passed on from one generation to the next. A couple where one or both of the partners has a family history of disease caused by faulty chromosomes or genes (genetic disease) may be anxious about the possibility of passing the problem on to any children they have. They may want to find out how likely it is to happen before choosing to start a family. If the woman is already pregnant the couple may want to know if the baby she is carrying has inherited a particular disease.

Examples of genetic diseases

Down's syndrome, cystic fibrosis and haemophilia are examples of genetic diseases that couples are likely to be concerned about.

Down's syndrome is the result of problems with whole chromosomes. People with Down's syndrome have an extra copy of chromosome 21. They are more likely to suffer from infectious diseases and heart problems and have difficulty speaking properly but with treatment are often able to work perfectly well day-to-day alongside other people.

Cystic fibrosis is the result of one faulty gene. A person suffering from the disease produces thick sticky mucus which particularly affects the lungs and intestines. Sufferers need regular physiotherapy and drugs to keep their bodies working.

Testing for genetic diseases

Today, it is routine for people who wish to have children to see if they are carriers of faulty chromosomes or genes. Usually a sample of blood is taken at the doctor's surgery and sent to a genetics laboratory, where the genes are analysed. Testing to find out if the baby developing in the womb is likely to be affected by a disease inherited from its parents is also routine. Two techniques are used to collect samples of the baby's cells for testing:

- **Amniocentesis**

  A thin hollow needle is used to draw off a sample of fluid from the womb (amniotic fluid). The fluid contains living cells from the baby. The cells in the sample are analysed for any defects in their chromosomes or in the genes the chromosomes carry.

- **Chorionic villus sampling**

  A small tube is gently pushed into the womb. Cells from the tissue that joins the developing baby to its mother are sucked into the tube. The cells are then analysed for genetic defects.

Giving advice

People who have reason to be worried about any genetic diseases they may pass on to their children can receive genetic counselling. Using the results of tests such as those described above, genetic counsellors can inform and advise people on decisions they need to make. But some people may want advice earlier than this, as the tests themselves raise

DIFFICULT DECISIONS

Here are circumstances that some people have to deal with when they know the results of genetic tests.

Couples where either one partner or both carry faulty genes can:
- start a family hoping that their children do not inherit faulty genes but if they do, be prepared to look after them
- start a family, but if testing shows that the developing child has inherited the faulty genes then end the pregnancy
- decide not to have children at all.

What other choices do you think that couples who carry faulty genes but who want children have?

Couples that have been told that their child will be born with a genetic disease may face the possibility that their child will die shortly after birth, or will live a healthy, normal life but probably die before reaching middle age. The parents-to-be can:
- end the pregnancy (abort the child) in all of the circumstances described
- end the pregnancy in only some of the circumstances
- have the child and hope that medical advances will help deal with any problems in the future.

What other factors do you think the parents-to-be should consider before making this difficult decision?

issues which may need to be thought about. Amniocentesis and chorionic villus sampling both slightly increase the risk of **miscarriage**. Chorionic villus sampling produces results for analysis four to six weeks earlier than amniocentesis. There would therefore be more time to decide what to do should the results indicate genetic problems ahead.

Many people think that parents-to-be should continue with a pregnancy even if tests indicate that the baby is at risk from genetic disease. Are there other choices to be made? How do you judge the value of a life, especially of someone suffering from incurable disease? There are no easy answers.

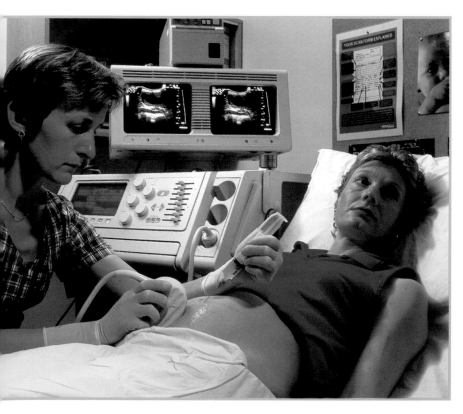

A doctor carrying out amniocentesis. The amniotic fluid is tested for chromosomal and genetic disorders such as Down's Syndrome.

Genetic engineering

All living things are made of cells, and all cells depend on **genes** to control the jobs they do (see page 6). **Genetic engineering** is possible because of the central importance of genes to the life of cells.

In the 1970s, scientists learnt how to alter the genetic make-up of cells. Genes could be moved from the cells of one type of **organism** into the cells of another type; for example between bacteria and plants or humans and yeast cells. Genetic engineering had arrived and new industries sprang into life driven by the methods of gene technology.

Why genetic engineering?

Cells are chemical factories, and genes are responsible for most of the chemicals that cells make. What scientists discovered is that a gene continues to control the production of the same chemical, even when moved from one type of cell into another type, and that this fact could be used to benefit humans.

For example, scientists found that they could chemically **synthesize** the sequence for making the human version of the **hormone** insulin. They made two **synthetic** genes, each coded for part of the insulin, then joined the parts together in a laboratory.

People who suffer from certain types of diabetes depend on insulin to stay healthy. Before genetic engineering, diabetics depended on insulin from cows and pigs. People with certain religious or **moral** beliefs, such as Hindus, Muslims, vegans and vegetarians, were prevented from using this insulin because of its animal origin.

Diabetes can be treated by a strict diet and the use of daily insulin injections.

INSULIN AND DIABETES

Insulin is a hormone produced by the pancreas (a gland near the stomach). It cuts down the level of sugar in the blood. Many diabetics have a pancreas that does not produce enough insulin. As a result their blood sugar increases to a level that may endanger health. Injecting insulin helps diabetics to control their blood sugar levels.

Is there a problem with genetic engineering?

Critics are concerned that genetically engineered bacteria will escape into the environment and cause havoc. They point out that escape is inevitable as no genetic engineering laboratory can be made 100 per cent safe. Also, once genetically engineered bacteria have escaped, they cannot be recaptured.

There is also concern that **genetically modified** organisms (GMOs) will make people ill and harm the environment. For example, in 1998 a soybean product had to be withdrawn from sale because it was found to contain genetic material from a Brazil nut which would cause a serious allergic reaction if eaten by people who have a nut allergy. However, there is currently not enough conclusive evidence to support these people's fears about GMOs.

Not everyone agrees that there is a problem with genetic engineering. The **biotechnology** industry has developed a genetically modified variety of rice that contains vitamin A. In developing countries such as China and India, many people suffer from a lack of vitamin A, which can cause blindness and weakens the immune system. The World Health Organization (WHO) estimates that a million children a year die from illnesses related to vitamin-A deficiency. The developers of this rice think it has the potential to help prevent many of these deaths.

What do you think? Could both groups be right? Is it worth taking the risk of genetic engineering if it saves lives? Or do you think there needs to be more testing?

CASE STUDY

The example of genetically engineered salmon raises the arguments both for and against this type of technology.

Economically, farming fish compares well with the production of meat from livestock reared using **intensive farming** methods. The fish are reared in moored cages underwater, and the farmers aim to control conditions so that the fish reach their weight for sale in the market as quickly as possible. To help the farmers, scientists have genetically engineered salmon so that the fish grow more quickly.

Wild salmon migrate long distances at sea before returning to their home rivers to breed. One approach is to use genetic engineering to stop the activity of the genes controlling migration. The captive salmon do not waste energy trying to swim long distances. The fish therefore grow more quickly and are ready for market earlier than their wild relatives. Another approach is to engineer the genes that control growth. Faster growth produces bigger fish which means more food more quickly (and more money for the farmer!)

Salmon often escape from fish farms. Would the escape of genetically engineered salmon have serious consequences? Scientists are still unsure. Genetically engineering salmon often includes trying to make sure that they will not breed with wild fish. However, the techniques are not completely effective.

What would happen if genetically engineered salmon were to escape and breed with wild salmon? What effect would it have on the environment? However, also remember that genetic engineering can help farmers to produce more food (including fish) to feed the world's growing population (see page 20).

Cloning

Have you ever cut off parts of the stem of a plant and put them into water to see if they sprout roots? If you went one stage further and planted the parts with sprouting roots into soil, you were probably rewarded with a group of healthy young plants. Did you know that your gardening activities had produced a group of plants containing the same genetic material as all of the others, including the parent plant? In other words the plants were genetically identical to each other. Living things which are genetically identical to each other are called clones.

Cloning plants preserves the characteristics of previous generations of plants in the offspring. In this way desirable qualities such as disease resistance, colour of fruit or shape of flower can be reliably reproduced in new stocks of plants.

Cloning animals like sheep and cattle is more difficult than cloning plants because no animal reproduces in the same way that plants do. Success depends on recent developments in **genetic engineering**. Today sheep, cattle, pigs, mice and other **warm-blooded** animals have been cloned, and their possible use for improvements in agriculture and medicine often makes the news headlines.

Cloning Dolly

Dolly the sheep became world famous because she was the first **mammal** to be cloned from an adult cell. How was Dolly produced?

FEMALE SHEEP 1: Udder cell is taken from an adult sheep.

FEMALE SHEEP 2: An egg cell is removed from a different adult sheep.

REMOVING THE NUCLEUS: Nucleus from egg is removed and discarded.

FUSION: Udder cell and empty egg cell are placed next to each other. A small electric current helps the nucleus from the udder cell pass into the empty egg cell.

DEVELOPING THE EMBRYO: Fused cell is **cultured** in a solution which contains all of the materials it needs to grow and divide. An embryo develops.

FEMALE SHEEP 3: Embryo is transferred to the womb of another sheep – the surrogate mother.

BIRTH OF THE CLONE: Surrogate mother gives birth to Dolly who is a clone of sheep 1. In other words, sheep 1 is Dolly's genetic (biological) mother even though sheep 3 gave birth to Dolly.

Cloning GM animals

Since the birth of Dolly in 1997 the debate about the benefits and dangers of cloning has gathered pace. Discussion is complicated by the development and use of **genetically modified** organisms in

Millie, Christa, Alexis, Carrel and Dotcom are the world's first cloned pigs. They have been produced by the same gene technology company responsible for cloning Dolly the sheep.

agriculture and medicine (see pages 22–3). If it is possible to clone animals like Dolly that are not genetically modified, then cloning ones that are is relatively simple. Look back to the flow diagram showing you how Dolly was produced. Substitute unmodified female sheep 1 with one that is genetically modified, and the way is open to produce clones of sheep (and other animals) all containing modified genetic material. How can we best judge the issues raised by cloning animals – genetically modified or not?

Benefits and dangers

One newspaper headline 'Warning on "human clones"' identifies a central issue. If it is possible to clone Dolly and other mammals then it should not be too difficult to clone people. Some people think the benefits could be enormous:

- Healthy cells taken from a sick person could be cloned and used to repair that person's damaged tissues

- The brain-dead clone of a person who would benefit from a **transplant** could be a source of matching organs for transplantation (see page 16). Because the organs of the person and his or her clone are genetically identical, there would be little risk of rejection of the transplanted organ.

Others point out the dangers:

- Most of us would be horrified at the thought of using brain-dead human clones as a source of organs for transplantation. The twin would have to be born at the same time since the clone would develop at the same rate as any other human. Otherwise by the time it was realized a transplant was needed it would be too late to grow a transplant clone.

These are some of the issues causing concern. As with most developing technologies, the benefits of cloning must be weighed against the dangers.

Testing medicines

Rights and wrongs

Is it right to use animals to test new medicines for the treatment of human illnesses? Most of us benefit from modern medicines. When we have a headache we may take a painkiller or if we have a sore throat we may go to the doctor for some antibiotics. However, some people rely on modern medicine every day of their lives. For example, millions of people worldwide suffer from diabetes. Their bodies do not produce enough insulin. The **hormone** insulin controls the body's blood sugar level and without it, the results can be fatal. Diabetics can now inject themselves with insulin to help maintain their blood sugar level but this is only possible because of experiments on animals.

Some people, however, think that benefits are not the issue. For them it is a question of **morals**. They think that using animals to test the effectiveness and safety of new medicines is cruel and wrong. Also, the claim is made that the human body is very different from the animal body. They argue that information obtained from testing the effects of a new medicine on animals cannot be used to predict the effects of the medicine on humans.

Forming opinions

Asking questions about every side of an argument helps shape opinions.

- Do we believe scientists when they say that testing on animals is vital for the development of new medicines?
- Why not use methods that do not involve animals to test new medicines?
- Can we condemn scientists who do the work?
- Are we glad of their work because modern medicines help cure diseases which had previously killed many people?
- Why should animals be made to suffer just for our benefit?

What are the facts about the use of animals for testing new medicines?

- The care of animals in laboratories and the way animals are used for research are strictly controlled by law.

Crowds protesting about the use of animals in research.

- Wherever possible, new drugs are tested in the laboratory on cells and tissues from humans and animals grown in solutions of all of the substances needed to keep them alive.
- Computers are helping scientists to design medicines on screen, so cutting down on the number of animals used for research.

Alternatives to animal testing

Finding alternatives to animal testing is not easy and takes a long time. There are many problems in finding out how effective or safe a new medicine might be. It is often the case that animal testing is the only available method scientists have to discover the answers to problems. There is progress but it is difficult to say whether animals will ever be completely replaced in the search for new medicines.

What do you feel about animal testing? Are there situations where you believe it is acceptable to test on animals?

FACTS

- *The number of experiments testing new medicines on animals has gone down by 50% in the last 30 years.*
- *Most tests on animals are carried out on rats and mice.*
- *About 0.4% of tests are carried out on cats and dogs.*
- *Less than 0.2% of tests involve monkeys and apes.*
- *The British Medical Association (the governing body for doctors) believes that animal tests are necessary to help doctors know how best to treat diseases. The Association also believes that alternative methods should be used whenever possible.*

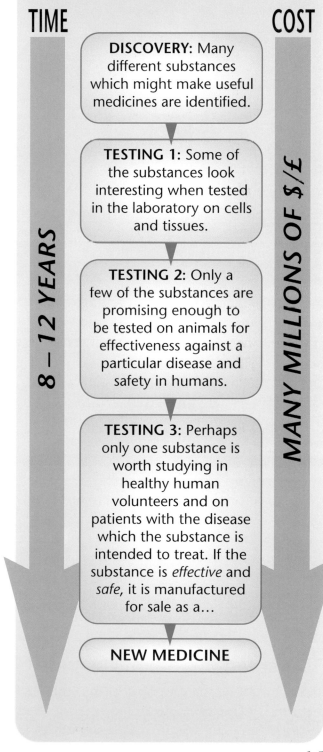

DISCOVERING AND TESTING NEW MEDICINES

Today there are more than 6000 different kinds of medicine available in Britain. Where do medicines come from?

TIME — 8 – 12 YEARS

COST — MANY MILLIONS OF $/£

DISCOVERY: Many different substances which might make useful medicines are identified.

TESTING 1: Some of the substances look interesting when tested in the laboratory on cells and tissues.

TESTING 2: Only a few of the substances are promising enough to be tested on animals for effectiveness against a particular disease and safety in humans.

TESTING 3: Perhaps only one substance is worth studying in healthy human volunteers and on patients with the disease which the substance is intended to treat. If the substance is *effective* and *safe*, it is manufactured for sale as a…

NEW MEDICINE

Animal organ donors

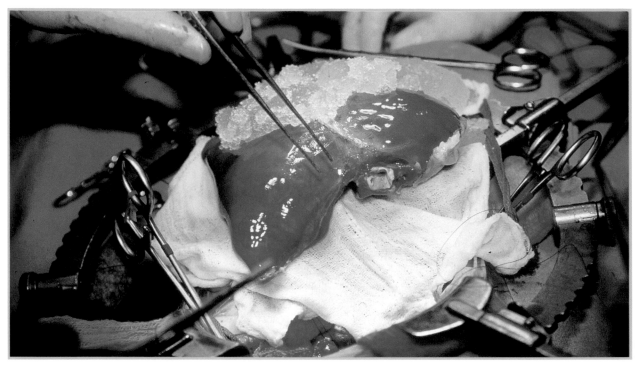

Transplant surgery aims to replace an **organ** that is not working properly with one that is. A donor is the person supplying the healthy organ and the person receiving it is the recipient. Most organ donors are victims of accidents. They have given permission for their organs to be transplanted. Some organ donors are alive, and give an organ where there are two in the body doing a particular job. For example there are usually two kidneys but one can do the job of filtering waste substances from the blood on its own, leaving the other available for transplanting into a person where both kidneys have stopped working. In these cases the donor and recipient are often members of the same family.

Transplanting animal organs

Unfortunately, the demand for human organs for transplantation far outstrips the supply. Also, the **tissues** of the donor and

Operations like this liver transplant can help to save lives. Unfortunately, demand for human organs is greater than supply.

recipient must be well matched if the surgery is to stand a chance of success. Otherwise the risk of the recipient's body rejecting the donated organ is increased. Drugs called immunosuppressants are often given to help to prevent the recipient's body from rejecting the donated organ.

The possibility of using animal donors was first explored in 1963 when American surgeons transplanted a kidney from a chimpanzee into a human patient. The transplanted organ was rapidly rejected by the recipient. It wasn't until the newly discovered technologies of **genetic engineering** opened the way to using **genetically modified** animals as organ donors that the matter was explored further.

PRODUCING GM ANIMALS

How are animals genetically modified to be suitable organ donors?

PRODUCING EGGS: Female animals are given **hormones** to make them produce lots of eggs.

DESIRED GENES: The human genes which protect our own organs from rejection (the desired genes) are identified and snipped out of **DNA**, using **enzymes** as 'molecular scissors'.

FERTILIZATION: The eggs are fertilized.

TRANSFERRING GENES: The desired genes are put into the nucleus of a fertilized animal egg. A number of fertilized eggs are treated in the same way. The eggs are genetically modified.

SURROGATE MOTHERS: Fertilized GM eggs are transferred to the womb of a female animal who is called the **surrogate** mother. There may be several surrogate mothers.

GM OFFSPRING: The surrogate mother gives birth to offspring each containing the desired genes. The offspring are genetically modified.

SUPPLYING ORGANS: The GM offspring grow up into adults, each containing organs protected from the risk of rejection.

MODIFIED ORGANS AVAILABLE FOR TRANSPLANTATION

As yet, however, the new techniques have not been used to give anyone an animal organ.

So, why GM? GM animals are not only a source of organs for transplant but might also be more effective donors if their organs can be altered to protect them from the risk of rejection by the recipient.

Pigs are preferred as a possible source of organs for transplantation because they have organs similar in size to humans. They are also easy to breed.

The issues

Using animals as a supply of organs for transplantation raises issues about the well-being of both animals and patients. Genetically engineering pigs to be animal donors should not mean that the pigs are treated any worse than those raised for human consumption. However, some people believe that genetically engineering animals is wrong because it shows a fundamental lack of respect for life.

Although the risk of infection from donor animal to recipient is small, the risk is real. It seems that cows infected with BSE (mad cow disease) are the cause of new variant CJD (the human form of the disease) in humans who have eaten infected meat. Should we use organs from donor animals to give critically ill people the chance of a new lease of life? Refusal may condemn such people to long-term illness or worse.

Using pigs as organ donors may also go against people's religious and cultural beliefs. For some people, pigs are considered 'unclean' and their religion prevents them from eating pig meat. Like many other people, they may feel that other approaches to solving the problem of the supply of organs are more worthwhile.

Intensive farming

There are more than twice as many people in the world as there were 50 years ago. How can farmers produce enough food for the world's growing population? Scientists and engineers have developed new technologies to help farmers in their work so that the land produces food in greater quantities. For example, chemicals are used to kill pests (insects, slugs, snails and fungi) that would otherwise damage food crops. Preventing damage means that there is more of the crop for people to eat.

In many parts of the world, machinery powered by fuel has replaced the muscle power of humans and animals, making the task of working the land more efficient. Greater efficiency means that more land can be used for farming and that crops are harvested more quickly.

A fleet of combine harvesters quickly cuts a field of wheat.

To increase the production of livestock (cattle, pigs and chickens) farmers crowd animals together in large buildings and feed them food that will help them gain weight. The lack of exercise and carefully controlled diet mean that animals grow more quickly and are ready to be killed for meat earlier than animals allowed to exercise freely outdoors. More meat means more food for people to eat.

Producing as much food as possible from the land available for raising crops and animals is called **intensive farming**. Why should intensive farming and the science and technology behind it raise issues that affect us all?

Problems with pesticides

Although insects are often thought of as nothing but pests – destroying plants and food – only a few types are a problem. The majority are harmless and some greatly benefit food production. We enjoy apples, plums and pears because bees transfer pollen between the flowers of fruit trees. Hungry ladybirds and hoverflies feed on greenfly and blackfly which would otherwise damage crops that are **staple** parts of our diet such as potatoes.

Unfortunately the **pesticides** used to kill insects (called **insecticides**) are very poisonous. They kill beneficial insects as well as insect pests and are a threat to the health of the farmers and other people who use them, unless they are handled very carefully. Also, some types of insecticide eventually seep into the water which collects underground (groundwater) and drains from the land into ponds and rivers. Groundwater and rivers are sources for much of the water we drink. Drinking water contaminated with insecticides can be a further threat to human health.

Destroying the environment

Modern farm machinery works best in fields without fences or other obstructions, so land is cleared of woods and hedges to make fields larger. However, the destruction of woods and hedges means that space for wildlife is also destroyed. With nowhere to live, farmland wildlife either dies out or moves away to seek refuge elsewhere. In England and Wales more than 200,000 kilometres of hedges have been removed from

Intensively reared pigs – new laws are intended to ease crowding, providing farm animals with better living conditions.

farmland over the past 50 years. As a result, the variety of wildlife found on modern farms has been much reduced.

Cruelty to farm animals

Is it fair for cattle, pigs, chickens and other farm animals to be crowded together indoors, so that we can enjoy eating more meat? After all, scientific evidence suggests that we need less meat in our diet than was thought 50 years ago. Cruelty to penned up animals involves physical discomfort, boredom and frustration. Some people argue that animals raised indoors must be content because they eat well and produce a lot of meat. However, we know that overeating in humans is a common sign of depression.

Intensive farming produces food in great quantities, and people should have enough to eat. However, arguments in favour of intensive farming must be set against the possible threats to human health, the damage its methods cause to the environment and the probable cruelty it inflicts on animals. Where do you think the balance lies?

Feeding the world

In the UK we do not need all of the food **intensive farming** methods produce. The crops, meat and dairy products not eaten have to be stored. In western Europe as a whole, food production has steadily increased since 1950 but the number of people has remained more or less the same. With so much food available, we eat more than we need. However, elsewhere in the world millions of people living in poorer countries do not have enough food to eat.

FACT

- *The human population is growing at an alarming rate. Today there are around 6000 million people living in the world. At the current rate of increase, the world's population could double by the year 2030.*

Shortage of food

People suffering from severe shortage of food (starvation) suffer serious physical effects. They become very thin, their skin becomes loose and dry, their muscles waste away, they lack energy and can only move slowly. If starvation continues for some time, there will be more serious damage to the body, until eventually the person dies from lack of food. Recovery from starvation comes from eating more food of the right sort, in appropriate quantities over a period of time.

While food goes to waste in the western world, elsewhere people starve.

Food aid

There is enough food in the world to feed everyone. Difficulties arise when food is not in the places where people need it most. Why don't we send our surplus food to the people of countries that need it?

Food aid may seem to be a sensible solution to world hunger. But…
- transporting massive amounts of food is difficult
- many of the people needing the food are scattered in remote rural locations
- it is difficult to ensure that the people who are really in need get the food

- flooding a country with food may destroy the area's economy. Local farmers may find it difficult to sell what little food they produce.

Organizations such as Oxfam have provided food aid in times of crisis like drought or floods. But does food aid provide a long-term answer to shortages of food? What other problems might there be?

Intensive farming

Intensive farming helps farmers produce large amounts of food. So should farmers be helped to develop intensive farming in countries where food is in short supply?

Yes, but...
- people in poorer countries cannot necessarily afford tractors or the fuel to run them. **Fertilizers** and **pesticides** are also expensive
- using the technology of intensive farming may not suit traditional methods of agriculture
- intensive farming can also cause damage to the already fragile environment
- if the extra food produced is not going to the local population but instead being exported to make money the situation has not improved.

Super-yielding crops

There is little point in sowing seeds if the crops growing from them do not produce very much food. For hundreds of years farmers have aimed to improve the yield of their crops. Rice, wheat, barley, rye, millet, maize and oats are the staple foods for most of the world's people. We know them as cereal crops. Scientists have worked especially hard to produce new varieties of high-yielding cereals.

For example, improvement in varieties of wheat is largely the reason why there has been an enormous increase in world production of wheat over the last 50 years.

The new varieties of crop may help farmers produce more food, but the seeds from which the super-yielding crops grow are expensive. How can farmers in poorer countries afford to buy them?

Scientists have **genetically modified** the crops to improve them. Developments include modifying crops to
- survive and flourish in places with low rainfall
- produce their own chemicals to kill insects which damage them
- resist diseases
- produce their own fertilizer.

Can we look forward to GM crops which grow in deserts, kill their insect pests and supply themselves with all of the nutrients they need for growth? The impact on food production in dry, hot, poorer countries would be immense.

However GM crops and the food that comes from them have stirred up a fierce debate in the UK and other countries worldwide. For countries short of food, where is the balance between improving food production to save lives through growing GM crops and the controversy that surrounds the technology?

Food aid, intensive farming and genetically modified crops seem to offer potential for feeding the world but politics, corruption, wars and the spread of deserts due to environmental damage add to the problems and interfere with the solutions.

21

GM crops

A GMO is a **genetically modified organism**. Stories about GM crops and the food that comes from them are newsworthy. Television shows us pictures of eco-activists tearing up fields of GM crops. Newspapers headline people's concerns about 'Frankenstein food' and possible damage to the environment. At first politicians supported the development of GM crops but, with protests mounting, they now voice fears about its safety. Why does GM food raise such passionate public debates?

The new technologies of **genetic engineering** allow scientists to cut out **genes** from the **chromosomes** of the cells of one organism and put them into the chromosomes of the cells of a different type of organism. We say that the organism with the 'foreign' genes has been genetically modified.

WHAT ARE GENES AND CHROMOSOMES?

If you look at cells under the microscope you can see tiny thread-like structures in the **nucleus** of each cell just before it divides into two. These thread-like structures are called chromosomes. Each one is made of lengths of a substance called **DNA** (short for deoxyribonucleic acid) coiled round a core of **protein**. Lengths of the DNA form genes. A gene is the code for making a protein. Each cell type has a different job to do depending on which of its genes are actively coded for making protein. Scientists use this information to modify organisms such as plants.

An eco-activist destroying a field of GM crops.

Producing more food

Even with **intensive farming** methods, feeding everyone is difficult for the reasons set out on page 20. Also, how are we to feed the many millions more that are expected to add to the world's population over the next thirty years. New approaches to food production are needed and genetically modified crops could help make the difference. Two case studies make the point.

CASE STUDY

Herbicide Resistance

Weeds are plants that compete with crops for what they both need: nutrients from the soil, space in which to grow and light for **photosynthesis**. The more weeds there are, the less well crops can grow, with the result that less food is produced. Herbicides are chemicals that kill weeds. However they can also kill crops, so farmers must use herbicides very carefully.

Not all plants are killed by herbicides. Some contain a gene that protects them from the effects, rendering them herbicide resistant. Through genetic engineering, scientists can introduce the gene for herbicide resistance into crop plants. Farmers can then destroy competing weeds with herbicides without harming the crop, making it easier for them to produce more food. However, a big worry is that these GM crops may **cross-fertilize** with their wild relatives, producing a weed that is resistant to herbicides.

Why are GM crops an issue?

What are the advantages of GM crops?
- The control of weeds and insects which reduce the amount of food produced is easier and safer for the farmer.

CASE STUDY

Insect Resistance

In some countries insects may destroy more than 30 per cent of the crops grown in a year. **Insecticides** are available, but have damaging consequences. The development of crops tolerant to damage by insects makes use of poisons produced by a type of bacterium that kills insects. Genetic engineering involves taking the gene for the poison from the bacterium and putting it into the cells of crop plants. The result – crop plants which kill the insects that try to eat them!

- The volume of chemicals used to control weeds and insects is reduced.
- The risk to wildlife and of damage to the environment is reduced.

Why then are people protesting about GM crops, when the advantages of their development seem clear-cut? First, people are worried that eating GM food might harm their health. They don't think there has been enough testing to prove it is safe. Next there are concerns that GM crops will harm wildlife. Finally, people are worried that transferring genes between organisms in the laboratory is somehow 'not natural'.

How can public opinion and scientific research work together to develop technologies that will help feed the world's ever-growing population? Perhaps there can be no meeting of minds. What then – starvation? What do you think? Do you think GM food is a good development? Does it need more testing? Or should it be banned completely?

Improving our food

Manufacturers put substances into our food to improve its taste, to make it look more attractive and to prevent spoilage. The substances are called food additives. The table below lists different food additives and what they do.

Much of our food is packaged in tins, tubs, bags and other containers which carry a label listing information about the food inside. The information includes the additives that are recognized as safe for us to eat. To make sure that they are safe to eat, each food additive is carefully tested. However, some additives that have passed the different safety tests can make some people ill.

Food additive	What each food additive does
Colourings	Make different foods good to look at
Flavourings	Make foods more tasty
Preservatives	Stop food turning bad
Driers	Remove water from food (e.g. flour) so that it 'runs' more easily
Emulsifiers	Mix together the oil and water which make sauces
Thickeners	Make food (e.g. soups) less runny
Supplements	Add nutrients such as vitamins A and D
Antioxidizers	Help prevent fats and oils turning bad

These sweets contain flavourings, colourings and emulsifiers. The table above explains why different additives are used.

What are the problems?

The public is concerned about the link between health risks and some additives, and this has put pressure on food manufacturers to stop using the additives even though they have been passed as safe. Food manufacturers fear that if they continue using these additives the public will stop buying the product. People are particularly worried about:

- tartrazine – colours different drinks and foods a bright yellow/orange. In some people it causes skin rashes, blurred vision, breathing problems and over-activity, especially in children.
- sulphur dioxide – used to stop certain foods from rotting. In some people it irritates the lining of the gut, causing pain and swelling.

However, cutting down on the amount of additives in our food may create new problems. Without preservatives the **micro-organisms** which turn food bad multiply much more quickly. Eating bad food causes food poisoning.

Food poisoning

In the UK since 1980 there has been at least a nine-fold increase in reported cases of food poisoning. The increase coincides with the growing public pressure to cut down on additives in food – but are the two linked? The increase could be the result of other factors:

- people have more money and are therefore eating out more
- ready prepared meals are increasingly popular
- more people are eating fast food
- food poisoning is reported more often because people are more informed about the symptoms.

The first three points are tied up with questions about the hygiene of places outside the home where food is prepared. The last point is to do with people being more aware of the food they eat and the hazards of eating bad food. None of the points can be linked to a reduction in the additives.

Irradiating food

Exposing food such as potatoes, mushrooms, chicken and spices to radiation – a process called irradiation – kills nearly all of the micro-organisms that cause food poisoning without making the food **radioactive**. Shops can keep irradiated food on the shelves for longer than untreated food, reducing waste and therefore costs. Shoppers can also keep the food at home for longer and therefore shop less often. It seems that everyone should be happy with irradiating food to help it keep longer.

However, the issue is not so straightforward. People are frightened of radioactivity. We know that radiation damages living **tissue**. We also know that exposure to radiation beyond the amount that we already experience from the environment increases the risk of the development of cancer.

However, the amount of radiation used to preserve food is tightly controlled. Food must not be sold for at least twenty-four hours after it has been irradiated. What is your opinion on the irradiation of food? Do you think it is necessary? Do the advantages outweigh the disadvantages?

Global warming and nuclear power

Have you ever been inside a greenhouse and noticed that it is much warmer inside than outside? It is no wonder that the plants grow well. The glass of the greenhouse absorbs the sun's rays and traps the heat they give off. In much the same way, carbon dioxide and water vapour in the earth's atmosphere work like the glass in a greenhouse. This is called the greenhouse effect. It raises the temperature of the Earth's surface. Without the greenhouse effect, life on earth as we know it would be impossible.

Steam billows from the cooling towers of a nuclear power station.

More carbon dioxide

As we burn coal, oil and gas (fossil fuels) in our homes, power stations and factories, we release huge amounts of carbon dioxide (a greenhouse gas) into the atmosphere. Millions of vehicles on the road burning petrol or diesel fuel add yet more. Our activities are probably putting too much carbon dioxide into the air to maintain the Earth's balance.

Is the increase in global temperature a direct result of the increasing levels of carbon dioxide? In the last one hundred years the Earth's surface has warmed up by 0.75°C. However, we know from historical records that the climate has been through extremes of cold and warmth before. Paintings from the 18th century show that winters were so cold that in England the River Thames was frozen. So-called 'frost fairs' were held on the sheet of ice.

Many scientists are convinced that global warming is the result of human activities releasing carbon dioxide into the atmosphere. At a conference in Kyoto in Japan in 1997, many countries agreed to reduce the release of carbon dioxide and other greenhouse gases into the atmosphere. Others, however, are more cautious. They cannot decide whether global warming is due to human activities or whether it is a natural variation in the Earth's climate.

Can nuclear power help?

Burning fossil fuels does more than anything else to increase the concentration of carbon dioxide in the atmosphere. In power stations fossil fuels are burnt to heat water. The steam produced drives huge turbines that generate the electricity which powers our homes and industry.

Switching from fossil fuels to nuclear power would massively reduce the amount of carbon dioxide entering the atmosphere. The reactions taking place at the heart of a nuclear reactor release enormous amounts of energy to heat water but no carbon dioxide. Nuclear-powered electricity would seem to be one way of solving the problems of global warming.

The problems of nuclear power

Nuclear power stations produce **radioactive** waste. The safe disposal of radioactive waste is a major problem for the environment and for us. Radiation is feared because it can alter the proper growth of cells, cause some types of cancer and increase the risk of women giving birth to deformed babies.

What are the risks to wildlife and human health if radioactive waste is accidentally released into the environment? What happens if there is an accident at a nuclear power plant?

The people in charge of the nuclear industry tell us that safety standards in the industry are high and that we are exposed to very little radiation from non-natural sources. But can we believe the reassurances?

CASE STUDY

Sellafield

Sellafield reprocessing plant is located on the coast in Cumbria, northwest England. Nuclear waste from the UK and other countries is sent there for safe disposal and to be turned into other materials, for example, plutonium for nuclear warheads. Over a period of 30 years there have been many accidents at Sellafield. Radioactive wastes have been released into the atmosphere and passed into the Irish Sea. The wastes are long-lived and will contaminate the environment for thousands of years.

Balancing the risks

Nuclear energy and fossil fuels underpin the industries that provide many people around the world with a standard of living never known before. People living in countries where living standards are not so good also want to improve their lot in life. They are unhappy about any agreements that might limit opportunities to develop their industries.

People's demands for lighting, heating, cars and other manufactured goods will increase the demand for fuel. The result will be the release of yet more carbon dioxide into the atmosphere, increasing the threat of global warming. If we choose the nuclear option, then more radioactive wastes will be produced and the risk of accidents will increase. It is a question of balancing the risks. Should developing nations be encouraged to try alternative natural energy resources, such as solar and wind power, first? But what if these sources don't meet their demands for power, or are too expensive?

Why conservation?

Ten thousand years ago about 12 million people lived in the world. Today the world's population is around 6000 million. People need food, homes, hospitals, schools... and many will want cars, televisions and computers among a vast range of other manufactured goods.

Humans are always making demands on their environment. We **exploit** the world's natural resources, such as fuels and metals, to make the goods we want and need. In the past these **non-renewable** resources have been used without much thought of what will happen when they run out, or the damage that occurs when they are used. However, people today are much more aware of these concerns.

Conservation means protecting the natural world against over-exploitation, pollution and other human pressures. Human well-being depends on keeping a balance between using and protecting environments and resources. Conservationists (people who work in conservation) aim to achieve this balance and care for the environment.

What is conservation?

Many people feel very strongly about conservation.

Organizations, such as Greenpeace and Friends of the Earth, inform people about different conservation issues and try to persuade governments to follow conservationist policies. Conservation involves different things for different people – from keeping the landscape beautiful to reducing energy consumption that relies on non-renewable resources.

What does conservation have to do with us?

It is not always easy to see why we should get involved in conservation. After all, in the UK most people have enough food, computers are everywhere and most homes have a television, washing machine and telephone. What are the links between our standard of living and events in other parts of the world?

One of the aims of conservationists is to protect areas of the countryside, like Epping Forest.

Extraction of many of the world's resources cause damage to the environment.

Our standard of living depends on using resources taken from the environment. The resources may not be from our immediate environment – indeed, many of the goods we need and want are made from metals that come from the world's poorest countries. For example:

- only two of the top ten copper-producing countries use large amounts of copper, the rest is exported to other countries
- only four of the top ten lead-producing countries use large amounts of lead
- of the ten top tin-producing countries, five are not leading tin users.

So, what do the figures mean? Developing countries that need resources (in this case, metals) for their own development are selling the resources to other countries that already have a far higher standard of living than their own. At the same time, the large-scale mining operations to extract the metals cause wide-scale damage to their environment.

Developing countries cannot afford to put the damage right and very often the mining companies extracting the metals think that the environmental damage is not their responsibility. They argue that the economy of the countries concerned benefit from the mining activities.

In fact, the money a country earns from sending its resources to other countries to be turned into manufactured goods is rarely enough to improve the living standards of its people. The people living near to the mines are actually exposed to increased pollution which can lead to health problems such as lead poisoning and **respiratory diseases**. In addition, turning resources into goods uses up valuable fuel energy.

FACTS

- *Of the world's population, 30% live in rich countries and use 85% of the world's fuel energy.*
- *The remaining 70% live in the world's poorest countries and use the remaining 15% of the world's fuel energy.*

Although all this may seem far removed from you, the copper wires that carry electricity to your house to power your television could well have come from a developing country. That is just one of many examples. What can you do to make a difference? By recycling your can of cola you are helping reduce the amount of new aluminium that needs to be mined. Can you think of other ways to make a difference? Every small action helps.

Immunization

Have you been immunized against different diseases? Immunization helps to prevent illness by using the body's own defences to fight infection. Smallpox was the first disease to be prevented by immunization. In 1796, country doctor Edward Jenner (1749–1823) tested his theory that people infected with the mild disease cowpox were protected from the similar but often fatal disease smallpox. In a series of experiments, Jenner deliberately infected a healthy boy, James Phipps, with cowpox and then later with smallpox. The experiment was very risky but James did not develop smallpox. His survival helped confirm Jenner's ideas.

Using a needle, Jenner scratched pus, taken from the spots of a person suffering from cowpox, into James' arm. Vaccines today are more sophisticated. Each one helps the body to resist a particular disease. The vaccines are either injected or swallowed – not painfully scratched into the skin!

How was James protected from smallpox? The cowpox pus stimulated his body's defences to resist the more serious smallpox. A modern vaccine works in the same way. A vaccine is a weakened or inactive form of a disease. When it is introduced into the body, the immune system fights it without the risk of serious illness. When the body encounters the active form of the disease, the body's defences are ready to fight it. In the case of smallpox, an international programme of immunization wiped out the disease by the end of the 1970s. In May 1980 the World Health Organization (WHO) was able to announce that the planet was free from the scourge of smallpox.

In the UK, the immunization of children to protect them from a range of diseases, follows a

Scratching substances, which helped prevent illness, into the skin was an early method of immunization. This painting shows Edward Jenner immunizing James Phipps by infecting him with cowpox.

schedule from the first year of life to the time of leaving school. Part of the schedule includes immunization against whooping cough. A programme of immunization against whooping cough started in 1957. Before then about 100,000 cases of the disease were reported in the UK each year. By 1973 more than 80 per cent of children had been immunized and the number of cases of whooping cough fell to around 2500.

Scare stories

Following a scare over the safety of the vaccine, the immunization programme suffered a serious setback and only about 30 per cent of children received the whooping cough vaccine in 1975. Outbreaks of whooping cough followed in 1977–79 and 1981–83 as scientists worked to make the vaccine safer and politicians tried to restore people's confidence. In 1986 about 68 per cent of children were immunized against whooping cough and further outbreaks of the disease were prevented.

The story of whooping cough illustrates how difficult it is to balance our individual freedom to choose what to do against what is good for everybody. The parents that did not have their child immunized against whooping cough decided that the chances of the child catching the disease (and the risks even if they did) were fewer than the risks of the child having the

FACT

● *For every 500,000 immunizations of whooping cough vaccine, fewer than 50 children experience some sort of side effect. Of these children, fewer than seven suffer serious complications. Without the immunization, 20,000 children would be at risk of dying.*

vaccine. Providing the proportion of children immunized against whooping cough is high enough, the minority who are not immunized are protected because they only meet children who have been immunized and are therefore not infectious. However, if the proportion of children immunized is low, an unimmunized child is more likely to meet another unimmunized child who is carrying the disease and become infected.

More recently another scare put the spotlight on the vaccine recommended to protect children against mumps, measles and rubella, all serious diseases. The vaccine for each disease is combined in one dose (MMR vaccine) and given as a single injection at 12–15 months of age.

In 1998 there were reports that soon after MMR immunization some children seemed to experience difficulties in their development. The number of children affected was small. However doctors were worried that parents would choose not to have their children immunized with the MMR vaccine, increasing the risk of the children catching serious diseases.

Despite reassurances, parents remained concerned and a further study was launched in 1999. No link was found between MMR vaccine and problems with children's development, and today most doctors think that the first report was just a coincidence.

Reading the scare stories helps you understand that there is no vaccine which protects everyone from a particular disease and is completely safe to use. It is all a question of balance. Is the risk from catching serious diseases greater than the risk of side effects from the vaccines which protect you from illness?

Fluoride and tooth decay

Dentists recommend that people brush their teeth with toothpaste containing calcium fluoride. This is because the hard enamel on the surface of teeth reacts with calcium fluoride to form an even harder covering that is better at resisting attack by mouth acids. These acids are produced when **microbes** in the mouth use sugar as food. People who eat sugary food and drink sugar-sweetened liquids are therefore more likely to suffer from tooth decay, and have a greater need for toothpaste with added fluoride.

The link between fluoride and healthier teeth was first made in 1901 by the dentist Fred McKay. He was working in Colorado, USA. Many of his patients had rusty-coloured stains on their teeth. Children's teeth were more affected than the teeth of adults. McKay called the symptoms 'Colorado Brown Stain' but could not find anything about the condition. He came to the idea that the staining was the result of something in the water that people were drinking. Among his patients McKay also noticed that those with stained teeth suffered less tooth decay than other patients. McKay wanted to find out why.

Finding the evidence

The search for evidence focused on the water supply of a number of towns. Scientists discovered that teeth became stained if there was more than two parts

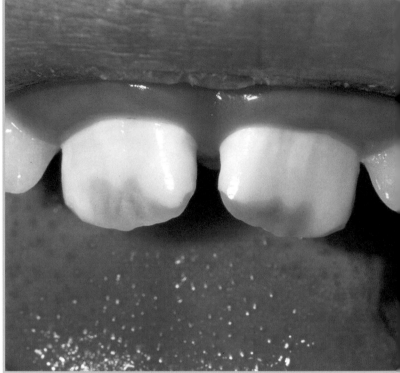

High levels of fluoride in drinking water cause permanent brown stains. They are part of the structure of the tooth enamel and cannot be brushed away.

per million of fluoride (see box) in the drinking water. Also children's growing teeth were more likely to be stained than adults' teeth. The 'something' in the water responsible for Colorado Brown Stain had been identified.

Other studies have shown the link between fluoride and a reduced risk of people suffering from tooth decay. For example, in 1945 a British dentist called Weaver compared the teeth of children living in North Shields and South Shields. The towns are in the northeast of England and located on opposite banks of the

River Tyne. The river runs into the North Sea. The drinking water for the people of North Shields contained between 0.2 and 0.3 parts per million of fluoride; for the people of South Shields the drinking water contained nearly 1.5 parts per million of fluoride. The children from North Shields had nearly 40 per cent more teeth affected by decay than the children from South Shields. The difference in the concentration of fluoride in the water supply of the two towns made the difference.

PARTS PER MILLION

Parts per million tells us how much of a particular substance is dissolved in a known volume of water. Imagine that among one million glass beads, two are red and all of the others are blue. We can say that there are two parts (red beads) per million parts (all beads). One part per million of fluoride is equivalent to one minute in two years – very little indeed!

Fluoridation

Eggs, milk, spinach and some types of tea contain fluoride, but only in very small amounts. We get most of our fluoride from the water we drink. Where the water is naturally high in fluoride, extra fluoride is not needed to keep people's teeth healthy. Where the level of fluoride in water is low, then brushing teeth with toothpaste containing fluoride successfully makes up the shortfall. In different parts of the world, small amounts of fluoride are added to drinking water where the level of natural fluoride is low. The process is called fluoridation. It increases the level of fluoride in water to around one part per million and is the cheapest and most effective way of preventing tooth decay.

Many different studies show that fluoridation of water is not a threat to good health. Yet, for all of its advantages, only about 250 million people worldwide drink fluoridated water (remember that the world's population numbers about 6000 million people). Why? For many people it is simply because they have difficulty finding clean water, let alone worrying about putting fluoride in it. However, for many people in developed countries there is concern that extra fluoride in drinking water increases their risk of developing cancer. People are also aware that if they are exposed to high levels of fluoride for a long time there is a risk of damage to bones, joints and the kidneys. However there is no risk to people's health from levels of fluoride up to one part per million: the standard by which water authorities measure the amount of fluoride (usually as sodium fluoride) added to drinking water.

Some people object to the idea of authorities adding fluoride to water without the permission of the people drinking the water. For them it is a question of the rights of individuals. They argue that no one should be forced into doing something (drinking fluoridated water) just because people in authority decide that it is a 'good' thing to do. Using toothpaste with added fluoride is different because the individual has a choice whether to use the toothpaste or not. Do you think that the rights of the individual are more important than a course of action that seems to be to everyone's benefit?

The body beautiful

The *Maja Clothed* by Francisco de Goya (1746–1828) may be a portrait of the Duchess of Alba. She was considered a great beauty of her day.

The media bombards us with images of the body that say 'thin is beautiful; fat is ugly'. However, comparison between the past and present shows how fashion trends shape our image of thinness and fatness. Most of the film stars of the 1940s were neither fat nor super thin. In the 17th and 18th centuries an even plumper body was fashionable.

Input versus output

A person's weight relates directly to their input and output of energy. The input of energy is in the form of food; output is all of the body's activities which keep the person alive using food energy to do so. For an adult, an input greater than output means weight gain; an output greater than input means weight loss; and when input and output are in balance, weight remains more or less constant. If a person eats more food than is required for his or her energy needs, then the excess is turned into fat and stored in fat cells under the skin. Gaining weight usually means gaining fat.

Companies that insure lives are interested in our health. Overweight people are more likely to be ill and are therefore a greater risk to insure. Life insurance companies have calculated healthy weights for people of different heights and body shape. For each height there is a range of weights which allow for differences in the size of the skeleton which forms the body frame. A large framed person will tend to weigh in at the upper limit of the weight range for a particular height; a small-framed person of the same height will tend to be at the lower end of the scale.

> ### FACT
>
> ● *People with well developed muscles may seem overweight for their height. Volume for volume, muscle weighs more than fat (we say that muscle is more dense). Providing they are fit, muscular people probably have less body fat than others of the same weight who do not take regular exercise.*

34

Slimming

Do you know someone who is on a diet to lose weight? At first weight is usually lost quickly. Most of the popular diets promoted by the multi-million pound slimming industry owe their success to sudden weight loss. However, this is mainly due to losses in body water and few people stick to a diet that demands major upheavals in their eating habits, so the weight soon goes back on. Nonetheless, encouraged by their early success weight watchers start again… and so on, trapped in a cycle of weight loss and weight gain.

Do many people really have a 'weight problem', or is it that the majority are just unhappy with their looks? Perhaps their unhappiness comes from the images of beauty pumped out daily by the media. Think also about the profits made by the companies that manufacture slimming diets. Does the industry have an interest in the continuing anxiety of people as they compare themselves with media images of super thinness?

Many people blame the media for the increased obsession with weight and appearance.

Eating disorders

Anorexia nervosa is an eating disorder which is on the increase in North America and the UK. It is not a simple case of taking slimming a bit too far. Anorexia is a psychological disorder – the sufferer feels that he or she is too fat and, repulsed by this fact, eats less and less, or refuses food altogether.

Anorexia is most common in teenage girls and young women, although 10 per cent of sufferers are boys. People with anorexia do not recognize that they are in effect starving themselves. Their opinion of themselves is low so treatment aims to boost confidence. If successful, normal eating patterns return and the person gains weight.

Bulimia is another eating disorder on the increase. Its victims eat large amounts of food (binge eating) and then rid themselves of the food – usually by making themselves vomit. In this way the person with bulimia avoids gaining weight. Again, self-image seems to be part of the problem. Improving the victim's view of themself and altering attitudes about food, eating and body image are important components of treatment.

Are eating disorders the result of society rating thinness too highly? Should the media take some responsibility? What do you think?

35

Sunbathing

Every year millions of people head for the seaside on holiday. Favourite beaches around the world are covered with bodies soaking up the sun. Relaxed and sun-tanned, most holiday-makers feel that the experience has been good for them.

Over the holiday period the newspapers and television often run stories warning people of the dangers of sunbathing. 'Cover up for healthy skin', 'Sunbathing increases the risk of skin cancer' are just a few of the headlines which alert us to the possible dangers of too much sun.

What is a sun-tan?

If skin is exposed to sunlight it changes colour. The change is what we call a tan. It can affect people in different ways, depending on their skin type. The change in colour or tan is the body's way of protecting itself from the burning and blistering effects of the sun's rays.

Beneath the surface of the skin lie cells filled with a pigment called melanin. When the sun's rays fall on the skin, the activity of the pigment cells increases and melanin enters the surrounding cells. The skin tans, filtering out the harmful rays which may damage the underlying layers of **tissue**.

The colour of skin

The colour of skin depends on the activity of its pigment cells. For example the cells are very active in people with dark skins. In people with fair (pale) skins the cells

Hundreds of people sunbathe on Bondi Beach in Australia.

are less active. How active the cells become is controlled by the person's **genes**. During the course of human evolution, **natural selection** meant that people living in hot sunny climates were at an advantage if the genes controlling the pigment cells of the skin were very active. A dark skin gives great sun protection. People living in cooler cloudier climates were not so much at risk. Selection for very active pigment cells was therefore less intense, resulting in fair skin. Trouble comes when naturally fair-skinned people sit out in the hot sun. Their pigment cells are less active. Even though the skin may change colour and tan, the protective effect is less than in those who have naturally dark skin.

> ## *FACT*
>
> ● *Pigment is the natural colouring in plant or animal tissue. The pigment in human skin that changes colour is called melanin. Melanin is brown to black in colour.*

Too much sun

Too much sun increases the risk of the skin's pigment cells becoming cancerous. The most serious type of skin cancer is a melanoma. Among fair-skinned people, melanoma is more common in those who are freckled, have blue eyes and fair hair, because their skin cells contain less melanin to protect them from the sun. What can they do to protect themselves?

Have you noticed that we have spoken about 'too much sun'? Some exposure to sunlight helps us to stay healthy. The sunlight converts a substance in the skin into vitamin D. We need vitamin D for

strong bones and teeth. In hot sunny countries, people make most of the vitamin D they need in this way. In countries where sunlight is reduced, people obtain most of their vitamin D from the food they eat.

Are there any benefits to sunbathing? Where do you think the balance lies between feeling better on the one hand and risking your health on the other?

Sunscreen cream has a sun protection factor which gives an idea how long it may be possible to be safely out in the sun before there is a risk of sunburn. Choice of sunscreen depends on skin type.

Smoking

Smoking cigarettes was the fashion at the beginning of the 20th century. Film stars glamorized smoking and advertising encouraged people to think about its supposed benefits. At the time, some doctors even thought smoking healthy and recommended it as a cure for depression. Most people didn't mind breathing in someone else's cigarette smoke and smoking was widely accepted in public places.

Today the approach to smoking could not be more different: smoking is banned in many public places, there are curbs on cigarette advertising and few stars of film, television or pop are seen smoking. What has brought about the change in attitudes to smoking?

Health risks

Smoking cigarettes means breathing in different substances in the smoke released by burning tobacco. Some of the substances help relieve tension and calm fears. These mood-altering effects of tobacco smoke helped to quickly establish the popularity of cigarettes – with the help of the addictive nature of nicotine!

However, scientific research has identified smoking cigarettes as one of the greatest causes of preventable death worldwide. Lung cancer, heart disease and emphysema are caused by smoking. The damage is done by various substances in tobacco smoke.

Marlene Dietrich was a famous Hollywood actress starring in many films during the 1940s.

- Nicotine is a powerful drug which is also addictive. It puts up the heart rate and blood pressure, increasing the risk of heart disease.
- Carbon monoxide is a gas which reduces the ability of blood to carry oxygen to the **tissues** and **organs** of the body. As a result the heart has to work harder to supply the parts of the body with oxygen. The harder work makes the heart more vulnerable to disease.
- Tar builds up in the lungs. It is a mixture of substances some of which cause cancer.

38

Smoking today

Although fewer people smoke cigarettes today than 30 years ago, many people still do. In fact, smoking is on the increase among young people, and teenage girls in particular. Parents, older brothers and sisters and other role models who smoke set the example which young people copy. Friends also copy each other to keep in with the crowd. This is the way smoking usually starts, and once hooked it is difficult to give up.

Although people may understand the risks of smoking cigarettes, health warnings on cigarette packets are often ignored and anti-smoking campaigns have little effect. For young people the risks of developing smoking-related diseases are no more than possible problems for the distant future. Older people may think that they have been smoking for so long that they can see little benefit in giving up something that they enjoy. Either way the different attitudes mean that people of all ages continue to smoke in spite of all the warnings of health risks.

What are the issues?

Do smokers have responsibilities to themselves and to others, knowing the risks to their health if they continue to smoke?

Should the government ban the sale of tobacco altogether? But what about the money that the government earns through taxes on cigarettes? Do individuals have the right to choose what they do to their own bodies? Do cigarette manufacturers have any responsibility for the health of their customers? Should the treatment of a smoker who has a self-inflicted illness be a lower priority than others? What do you think?

FACTS

- *Each year in Britain about 120,000 people die young because they smoke.*
- *At today's prices some estimates put the cost each year to health services of treating smoking related diseases in the UK at about £1.6 billion.*
- *Non-smokers suffer increased risks of ill health when they breathe in smoke from other people's cigarettes – known as 'passive smoking'.*
- *Babies born to mothers who smoke weigh less on average and suffer more health problems than babies born to non-smokers. Passive smoking also affects the unborn child.*

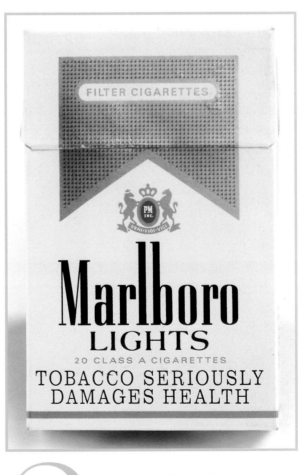

FILTER CIGARETTES

Marlboro
LIGHTS
20 CLASS A CIGARETTES
TOBACCO SERIOUSLY DAMAGES HEALTH

Warnings against smoking-related diseases appear on all cigarette packets.

Contraception

Family planning

If a couple want to have sexual intercourse, and do not want to have a baby, then they use some form of contraception. Choosing when to have children is called family planning or birth control. To prevent pregnancy, the method of contraception must either stop sperm from reaching the egg, stop eggs from being produced or stop the fertilized egg from developing in the woman's womb. Scientists have developed a number of contraceptive devices. The table lists different methods of contraception and how they work.

Why contraception?

Many people believe that contraception should be freely available and that choosing to use contraception is a basic human right. They argue that the act of sexual intercourse gives expression to people's sexual and emotional needs and that satisfying these needs should not carry the risk of pregnancy.

Contraceptives for both men and women.

Method of contraception	How the contraceptive works
Male condom (sheath) – unrolls over the penis ....Stops sperm from	
Female condom – fits around the vagina	reaching the egg
Foams and creams...Kills sperm	
Diaphragm or cap – fits over opening to the womb ....Prevents sperm from entering the womb	
Hormone contraceptives – usually in the form.......Stops eggs from being produced of 'the pill'	
Coil (often of copper wire) – fitted inside the....................Stops fertilized eggs from woman's womb	developing in the womb

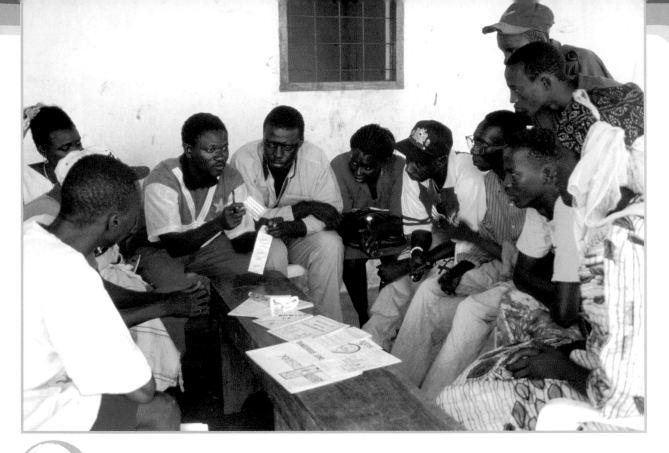

Health workers in the Gambia provide advice and information about family planning.

The world's population stands at around 6000 million people, and the numbers are growing at an alarming rate. In fact the growth rate of the human population in some parts of the world is so great that the countries concerned have government-sponsored campaigns to encourage people to use contraception to limit the size of their families. Indeed in some places there are legal penalties for couples who have more than one child.

Safe sex is another reason often given in favour of using contraception. Condoms stop the spread of diseases which can pass from person to person during sexual activity. Syphilis and gonorrhoea, which are caused by different types of bacteria, are examples. So too is AIDS (see pages 42–3), which is caused by the human immunodeficiency virus (HIV).

What are the issues?

Many people believe that it is wrong to use contraception because of their religious views. They argue that contraception contradicts the word of God set out in holy scriptures. Some say that it is unnatural.

Others say that contraception encourages people to have numerous sexual partners. They point out the increased risks to health. Also, they believe that having sex becomes a casual activity and undermines people's ability to form long-lasting, loving relationships. In North America there is growing support for the slogan 'Say No'. The campaign argues that saying no to sex outside marriage is the best way to protect people's sexual health and to support families. Saying no is, of course, the safest and surest form of contraception. What do you think?

HIV and AIDS

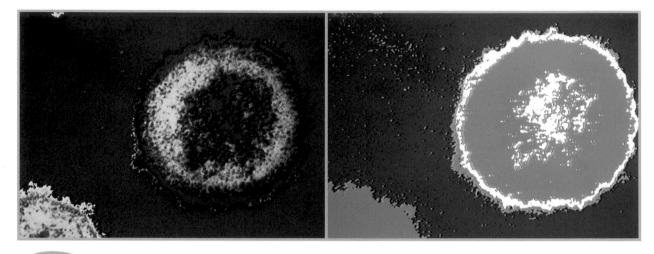

This image of human immunodeficiency virus (HIV) is magnified many times. Like all viruses, HIV consists of a strand of genetic material within a coat of **protein**. Viruses are not 'alive' in the sense that they do not need food as a source of energy, and they can only reproduce after infecting a cell.

AIDS stands for Acquired Immune Deficiency Syndrome. It is caused by the human immunodeficiency virus (HIV) which attacks the cells in the blood that help us fight disease. The cells are an important part of the immune system, which keeps most of us healthy for most of the time. Infection by HIV weakens the immune system. As a result people infected with HIV do not suffer from the effects of the virus itself. Their illness is the result of the different diseases which gain a foothold after HIV has destroyed sufficient numbers of the blood cells of the immune system.

How does HIV affect the body?

After infection, a person may feel unwell for a short time. The symptoms are rather like those of flu, but the person soon recovers. A long period (up to ten years) may follow when there are few signs of illness. During this time (the incubation period) the person is HIV-positive and able to pass on the virus to another person, often without knowing it.

When HIV has destroyed sufficient numbers of the cells of the immune system, the symptoms of AIDS appear. Diseases that a healthy immune system would normally control take hold. Different types of cancer, weight loss, diarrhoea and fever are common. Treatment with different types of drug may delay the onset of disease, but AIDS eventually develops in most HIV patients with fatal results.

The spread of AIDS

AIDS was first reported in the USA in 1981 among homosexual men who previously had enjoyed good health. It was already widespread in Africa. Now AIDS is seen worldwide, and about 19 million people are estimated to have died of the disease, including nearly 4 million children born to mothers infected with HIV.

As well as those who have died, about 35 million people worldwide are thought to be infected with HIV. In some of the worst affected countries, up to one quarter of the adult population is infected, which in the near future will result in possibly 24 million more deaths. The cost is not only in wasted lives but in the social and economic fabric of society itself. How do you think the spread of AIDS could affect the organization and running of a country?

Preventing infection

HIV can be passed from person to person during unprotected sexual intercourse (that is, without the protective barrier of a condom), or when addicts share syringes and needles to inject drugs, or from an HIV-infected mother to her baby, or from blood transfusions with infected blood. Different advertising campaigns highlight the threat from HIV infection through unsafe sex and drug abuse.

The issues

Each year tens of millions of pounds and dollars are poured into research to find new treatments for AIDS and to slow down the spread of HIV. The threat to health is serious, as the figures show. However, does the effort put into AIDS research mean that programmes investigating ways of treating other diseases are starved of funds? Think of the figures:

- Around 2400 million people are at risk from malaria and 2 million die from the disease each year
- In developing countries, 4 million children die each year from the effects of diarrhoea
- In North America and Europe, cancer accounts for 15 per cent of all deaths.

Throughout history humans have been affected by 'high profile' diseases, and the way society responds to them. Think of smallpox in the 17th and 18th centuries (see page 30) and more recently polio. Is AIDS another example of a high profile disease which is taking away money from research into other less exciting but equally threatening illnesses? Or is it worthwhile spending this amount of money to save the millions of people affected? What are your views on the issues?

Elizabeth Taylor is one of a number of film stars supporting charities that raise funds for AIDS research.

Glossary

ancestors organisms that other more recent organisms (descendants) can be traced back to

biotechnology the way in which we use plant cells, animal cells and microbes to produce substances that are useful to us

blueprint literally, a blue photographic print of building plans; the word is often used more generally to mean a detailed plan or scheme

chromosomes tiny rod-like structures found in the cell nucleus. Each chromosome consists of deoxyribonucleic acid (DNA) wound round a core of protein.

cross-fertilize the joining (fusion) of sperm and eggs from different individuals

cultured growing microbes or tissues in a solution of all of the substances needed for their growth

DNA short for deoxyribonucleic acid, a substance that combines with protein to form the chromosomes in the cell nucleus. Lengths of DNA on each chromosome form genes.

enzymes proteins formed in living cells that help chemical processes, such as the digestion of food, to occur

exploit to make use of something for profit or personal gain

fertilizer substance added to soil to help plants grow

genes lengths of DNA, each coding for the production of a protein by a cell

genetically modified (GM) refers to an organism that has had genes from a different type of organism transferred into it

genetic engineering processes used to identify and insert genes of one type of living thing into the DNA of the cells of another (different) type of living thing

hormones chemicals produced and released by different tissues into the bloodstream. Hormones usually affect tissues in the body some distance from the place where they are produced and released.

insecticide type of pesticide used to kill insects

intensive farming producing as much food as possible from the land available for raising crops and animals

mammal warm-blooded animal whose body is covered by hair and whose young are fed on milk produced by the female

microbes also called micro-organisms

micro-organisms organisms that are microscopic (only visible under a microscope), such as bacteria and viruses

miscarriage when a foetus developing in the womb dies before birth and is discarded from the body

molecules two or more atoms combined together; if the atoms are the same it is an element, if they are different it is a compound

moral the distinction between right and wrong

natural selection process that favours the individuals in a group with the features that best suit them to survive. Less well suited individuals leave fewer offspring or die before they can reproduce.

non-renewable refers to something that can be completely used up

nucleus the positively charged core of an atom

organ a group of tissues doing a particular job

organism any living thing

patents a legal document which registers a person's (or organization's) ownership of an invention so that other people cannot use the invention without the owner's agreement

pesticide chemical used to kill pests

photosynthesis the chemical reactions in plant cells that use the light energy trapped by the green pigment chlorophyll to convert carbon dioxide and water into sugars and oxygen

proteins a group of complex compounds that are essential for all living things

radioactive something that gives off radioactivity is said to be radioactive. There are three types of radioactivity: alpha radiation, beta radiation and gamma radiation. The different radiations come from the nuclei and electrons on atoms.

respiratory disease disease that affects breathing

shareholder person who invests money in an organization and who is issued with 'shares' that register the amount of money invested. Shares are traded in the stock exchange and may go up or down in value. The shareholder will hope to receive a dividend (profit) each year on the amount of money originally invested.

staple refers to a type of food that is central to the diet of a country

surrogate substitute

synthesize/synthetic make something (that consists of several parts) by combining substances together; something that is synthetic is made by synthesis

tissue a group of similar cells working together to do a particular job

transplant the transfer of tissues or organs from one part of the body to another part of the same individual or that of another individual

warm-blooded having a temperature at the centre of the body that remains steady even though the temperature outside changes. Humans are warm-blooded. So too are birds and all other mammals.

Contacts and helplines

BLAKE SHIELD BNA TRUST
PO Box 5681, Rushden
Northants
NN10 8ZF
www.bna-naturalists.org/

THE BRITISH MEDICAL ASSOCIATION
BMA House, Tavistock Square
London
WC1H 9JP
web.bma.org.uk

THE FIELD STUDIES COUNCIL
Information Office, Preston Montford
Montford Bridge, Shrewsbury
Salop
SY4 1HW
web.ukonline.co.uk/fsc.dalefort

MINISTRY OF AGRICULTURE, FISHERIES AND FOOD
Nobel House, 17 Smith Square
London
SW1P 3JR
www.maff.gov.uk

THE NATURE CONSERVANCY COUNCIL
Northminster House
Peterborough
PE1 1UA

ROYAL PHARMACEUTICAL SOCIETY OF GREAT BRITAIN
1 Lambeth High Street
London
SE1 7JN
www.rpsgb.org.uk

ROYAL SOCIETY FOR NATURE CONSERVATION
The Green, Nettleham
Lincoln
LN2 2NR

In Australia

AUSTRALIAN AND NEW ZEALAND COUNCIL FOR THE CARE OF ANIMALS IN RESEARCH AND TEACHING
The Director, PO Box 19
Glen Osmond SA 5064
Australia
61-8-8303 7393
Email: anzccart@waite.adelaide.edu.au
www.adelaide.edu.au/ANZCCART/

AUSTRALIAN GENE ETHICS NETWORK
340 Gore St, Fitzroy VIC 3065
Australia
(03) 9416 2222
Email: info@geneethics.org
www.geneethics.org/

CSIRO
CSIRO Enquiries , Bag 10
Clayton South VIC 3169
1300 363 400
Email: enquiries@csiro.au
www.csiro.au/

FRIENDS OF THE EARTH
312 Smith Street Collingwood
PO BOX 222, Fitzroy 3065 Australia
9419 8700
Email: foe@foe.org.au
www.foe.org.au

GREENPEACE
GPO BOX 2622
Sydney NSW 2001
www.greenpeace.org.au

RSPCA AUSTRALIA
PO Box E369
Kingston ACT 2604
(02) 6282 8300
Email: rspca@rspca.org.au

Further reading

Medical Advances
S Parker
Hodder Wayland 1997

Microlife: Scientists and Discoveries
Robert Snedden
Heinemann Library 2000

Success at Key Stage 3: Science
E Ramsden, D Applin and J Breithampt
Hodder and Stoughton 1998

Turning Points in History: Penicillin
Richard Tames
Heinemann Library 2000

Twentieth Century Science and Technology
Steve Parker
Heinemann Library 2000

What's at Issue: Animal Rights
Paul Wignall
Heinemann Library 2000

What's at Issue: Health and You
Julie Johnson
Heinemann Library 1999

What's the Big Idea: Genetics
M Brookes
Hodder Children's Books 1998

What's the Big Idea: The Mind
N Barber
Hodder Children's Books 1996

Index